C000071120

Supporting Spelling

FOR AGES 12–13

Contents

Introduction

The *Supporting Spelling* series is aimed at all those who work with students who have been identified as needing 'additional' or 'different' literacy support. It can be used by anyone working with students who fall into this category, whether you are a teacher, classroom assistant or parent.

Typically, the twelve to thirteen year-old students, for whom the book is intended, will be working at the levels expected of Year 6 or Year 7 pupils or they may simply need extra help in tackling the level of work appropriate for Year 8. Their difficulties may be short-term, and overcome with extra practice and support on a one-to-one or small group basis, or they may be long-term, where such support enables them to make progress but at a level behind their peer group.

The activities in this book provide exactly what these students need – plenty of repetition and practice of spelling skills, based on close observation of words together with listening to the sounds within words. The students are encouraged to say the words and to listen to both the syllables and the phonemes from which the words are formed. Some students reach a level of maturity at the early secondary school stage where they can apply a 'retrospective phonics' approach to words, understanding the links between sounds and graphemes possibly for the first time. Within this book we provide an approach that is:

> Systematic
> Multi-sensory
> Based on Speaking and Listening
> Linked closely to reading skills

This book is organised into double page spreads. Each spread consists of a page of teachers' notes introducing specific words followed by a worksheet containing activities centred around these words. All the activities can be used on their own or alongside other literacy schemes that are already established within the school. The activities are simple and self-explanatory and the instruction text is kept to a minimum to make the pages easy to use for adults and less daunting for students to follow. Suggestions for additional activities are supplied if appropriate.

The words featured in this book are drawn from:

(i) the high and medium frequency words recommended for primary aged students;
(ii) vocabulary suited for students at the early part of secondary school;
(iii) lists of words that contain particular prefixes, suffixes, inflections and letter strings recommended for students at the early part of secondary school.

Students generally achieve the greatest success in an atmosphere of support and encouragement. Praise from a caring adult can be the best reward for the students' efforts. The worksheets and activities in this book will provide many opportunities for students to enjoy these successes. The development of a positive attitude and the resulting increase in self-esteem will help them with all of their schoolwork.

Record and Review

Name: _____ Date of birth: _____

Teacher: _____ Class: _____

Support Assistant: _____

Code of Practice stage: _____ Date targets set: _____

Target

1 _____

2 _____

3 _____

4 _____

Review

Target

1 _____

_____

_____ Target achieved? ☐ Date _____

2 _____

_____

_____ Target achieved? ☐ Date _____

3 _____

_____

_____ Target achieved? ☐ Date _____

4 _____

_____

_____ Target achieved? ☐ Date _____

Definitions and explanations of terms

Many documents use terminology that is unfamiliar to non-specialists and some definitions are listed below. Please note that some publications will give slightly different definitions.

Antonym   An antonym is a word that is opposite in meaning to another word, eg 'hot' and 'cold'. An antonym prefix is a prefix that creates a word that is opposite in meaning to another: e.g. 'un' added to 'necessary' creates 'unnecessary'.

Homonym   A homonym is a word having the same sound or spelling as another but which has a different meaning e.g. the word 'bow' can be the front of a boat or it can be the act of bending forward when an audience is applauding. But the word 'bow' with a different sound, as in a ribbon tied in a bow, is still a homonym.

Homophone   A homophone is a word having the same sound as another word but with different meaning or spelling e.g. the words 'bear' and 'bare' are homophones.

Inflection   An inflection is a suffix that is used to change a word to show tense, gender, number, etc. e.g. 'ed' is an inflection that can be added to a word to change its tense: 'climb' – 'climbed'.

Prefix   A prefix can be placed at the beginning of an existing word to change its meaning e.g. 'dis' can be placed at the beginning of 'advantage'.

Suffix   A suffix can be placed at the end of an existing word to change its meaning e.g. 'al' can be added to the end of 'music'. (Note, out of interest, that the 'ic' in 'music' is itself a suffix that was incorporated into the Greek word mousike, meaning 'of the Muses'. Thus words such as epic, critic and music can all be said to have the suffix 'ic' although the suffix has not been added to a modern word.)

Synonym   A synonym is a word that means the same or nearly the same as another word e.g. 'jump' and 'leap'.

The following definitions and explanations all relate to terminology used in relation to phonics.

Phoneme	A phoneme is a unit of sound and can be represented by: one letter, e.g. **b** as in **b**at two letters, e.g. **ee** as in sw**ee**t three letters, e.g. **ear** as in n**ear** Note that a phoneme (a sound) can be represented in several ways e.g. the sound /ee/ can be represented by: **ee** as in f**ee**t **ei** as in c**ei**ling **ie** as in ch**ie**f **ea** as in n**ea**t **i** as in sk**i** **e_e** as in P**ete**
Vowel phoneme	A vowel phoneme makes an open sound and always contains at least one vowel – you usually have to open your mouth to say it. Examples of vowel phonemes are: /a/ as in b**a**t /ie/ as in cr**ie**s /oo/ as in b**oo**k /ur/ as in t**ur**n /ow/ as in t**ow**n
Consonant phoneme	A consonant phoneme always contains at least one consonant and usually involves closing the mouth, or 'biting' the lower lip, or touching the roof of the mouth with the tongue. (There are exceptions, e.g. /h/). Examples of consonants phonemes are: /b/ as in **b**at /f/ as in **ph**otograph /th/ as in **th**ey /ng/ as in si**ng**
Grapheme	A grapheme is a letter or pair of letters or group of letters representing a single sound e.g. **ee**, **ei**, **ie**, **ea**, **i** and **e_e** are all graphemes representing the sound /ee/.
Grapheme/phoneme correspondence	The relationship between letters and the sounds that they represent.

Digraph	A digraph consists of two letters representing a single sound. So, for example, the grapheme **ch** is a consonant digraph because it is made up of two consonants. The grapheme **ee** is a vowel digraph, but **ow** is also a vowel digraph, although it contains a consonant, because it makes an open sound like a vowel does.
Split digraph	A split digraph consists of two vowels separated by a consonant to make one phoneme e.g. **e_e** as in Pete **i_e** as in mine **a_e** as in came
Trigraph	A trigraph is a group of three letters representing a single sound. The vowel phonemes /air/ and /ear/ are trigraphs.
Cluster	A cluster consists of two or more letters making more than one sound e.g. **t h r** are three letters that can make the cluster **thr**, which consists of the phonemes /th/ and /r/.
Blending	Blending is the process of combining different sounds (phonemes) to be able to say a particular word or to make up part of a word e.g. /sh/ /i/ /p/ can be blended to make the word ship. /th/ /r/ are blended to make the cluster **thr**. Sometimes a cluster like this will be called a blend.
Segmenting	Segmenting is the process of splitting a word into its different phonemes to be able to spell the word e.g. **ship** can be segmented into the three phonemes /sh/ /i/ /p/.
vc	vowel/consonant, e.g. the word *it*
cv	consonant/vowel, e.g. the word *be*
cvc	consonant/vowel/consonant, e.g. the word *cat*
ccvc	consonant/consonant/vowel/consonant, e.g. the word *shop*
cvcc	consonant/vowel/consonant/consonant, e.g. the word *fast*

An introduction to phonemes

Language can be analysed by considering the separate sounds that combine to make up spoken words. These sounds are called phonemes and the English language has more than forty of them. It is possible to concentrate on forty-two main phonemes but here we list forty-four phonemes including those that are commonly used only in some regions of the country.

It is helpful to look at each phoneme then at some sample words that demonstrate how the phoneme is represented by different graphemes, as shown in the list below. Try reading each word out loud to spot the phoneme in each one. For the simple vowel sounds the graphemes are shown in bold text.

Vowel phonemes	Sample words
/a/	b**a**t
/e/	l**e**g, gu**e**ss, h**ea**d, s**ai**d, s**ay**s
/i/	b**i**g, plant**e**d, b**u**sy, cr**y**stal, d**e**cide, **e**xact, gu**i**lt, r**e**peat
/o/	d**o**g, **ho**nest, w**a**s, qu**a**rrel, tr**ou**gh, v**au**lt, **ya**cht (the ch is silent)
/u/	b**u**g, l**o**ve, bl**oo**d, s**o**me, c**o**mfort, r**ou**gh, **yo**ung
/ae/	rain, day, game, navy, weigh, they, great, rein
/ee/	been, team, field, these, he, key, litre, quay, suite
/ie/	pie, high, sign, my, bite, child, guide, guy, haiku
/oe/	boat, goes, crow, cone, gold, sew, shoulder
/ue/	soon, do, July, blue, chew, June, bruise, shoe, you, move, through
/oo/	book, put
/ar/	barn, bath (regional), laugh (regional), baa, half, clerk, heart, guard
/ur/	Thursday, girl, her, learn, word
/or/	born, door, warm, all, draw, cause, talk, aboard, abroad, before, four, bought, taught
/ow/	brown, found, plough
/oi/	join, toy, buoy
/air/	chair, pear, care, where, their, prayer
/ear/	near, cheer, here, weird, pier

Try saying this vowel phoneme:

/er/	fast**er**, g**a**zump, curr**a**nt, wooll**e**n, circ**us**

Not to be confused with the phoneme /ur/, this phoneme is very similar to /u/ but is slightly different in some regions.

Consonant phonemes	Sample words
/b/	bag, rub
/d/	dad, could
/f/	off, calf, fast, graph, tough
/g/	ghost, girl, bag
/h/	here, who
/j/	bridge, giraffe, huge, jet
/k/	kite, antique, cat, look, quiet, choir, sock, six (note that the sound made by the letter x is a blend of the phonemes /k/ and /s/)
/l/	leg, crawl, full
/m/	mug, climb, autumn, sum
/n/	now, gnash, knight, sign, fun
/p/	peg, tap
/r/	run, wrote
/s/	cinema, goose, listen, psalm, scene, see, sword, yes, less
/t/	ten, sit, receipt
/v/	vest, love
/w/	wet
/wh/	when (regional)
/y/	yes
/z/	choose, was, zoo
/th/	the, with
/th/	thank, path
/ch/	cheer, such, match
/sh/	shop, rush, session, chute, station
/zh/	usual
/ng/	thing, think

For some phonemes you may dispute some of the examples that we have listed. This may be due to regional variations in pronunciation. Disputing the sounds is a positive step as it ensures that you are analysing them!

It is certainly not necessary to teach the students all of the graphemes for each phoneme but to be ready and aware when they suggest words to you to represent a particular sound. They are not wrong with their suggestions and should be praised for recognising the phoneme. You can then show them how the words that they have suggested are written but that normally the particular sound is represented by a specific grapheme.

Words from the school timetable

1 Focus on words

● Photocopy this page and the accompanying student worksheet. Discuss the focus words at the bottom of this page with the students. (You may decide to change one or two to reflect the timetable used in your school.) Ask the students to write the words in the blank grid on their worksheet. You could dictate the words or, if appropriate, students could copy them from the set below.

● The completed grid on the worksheet, or the one below, could be laminated as a pocket reference card that students could refer to later.

● To analyse the words further, and if appropriate for your students, you could complete the following activities.

Segmenting the words into their phonemes

This is not an easy activity but the process encourages students to listen closely to the sounds that constitute the words. Explain to the students that they are going to segment some of the words into their separate sounds. Demonstrate this with the word *music* by drawing lines between the graphemes that represent the separate phonemes: /m/u/s/i/c/. Now look at *design*: /d/e/s/ig/n/. Encourage the students to notice that the letter **g** is not sounded and can be called a 'silent letter'. Ask the students to try some of the other words. They may come up with different answers from each other but the important part of the activity is the process of hearing the separate sounds and observing how they are represented by graphemes. Some words are particularly difficult to analyse in this way but this helps to draw attention to their particular letter strings. In the word *education* the students might find it difficult to decide how to segment the phonemes in **tion**. Through this they can learn that the letter string **tion** can be broken down into the phonemes /sh/u/n/.

Splitting the words into their syllables (syllabification)

For most students syllabification is much easier than segmenting. Explain that they are now going to split the words into 'chunks' of sound and give the example of *communication*: \com\mu\ni\ca\tion\. Can the students hear that the word can be split into five syllables? Point out that each syllable normally contains at least one vowel.

2 Words in context

● When the students are ready ask them to complete the second activity on the worksheet in one of two ways. They can either attempt to read the sentences and write the missing words or they can listen to you dictating the sentences and write the missing words as you dictate them.

● As an extension activity, have a blank timetable ready to discuss with the students. They could use this to try to show their own timetable as accurately as possible or they could be more creative e.g. they could design their ideal timetable according to set criteria such as: there must be at least one foreign language and all the other subjects must appear at least once.

Art	Music	Assembly	History
Geography	Science	Mathematics	Design
Technology	Citizenship	English	Physical Education
French	German	Spanish	Religious Education
Drama	Information	Communication	Personal, Social, Health

Words from the school timetable

Name _____

1 Write the focus words in the spaces on this grid.

2 Complete the following sentences.

French, _____ and _____ are modern foreign languages.

The letters PSHE are short for _____ , _____ and

_____ Education.

The letters PE are short for _____ Education.

The letters ICT are short for _____ and _____

_____ .

The letters DT are short for _____ _____ .

The whole school goes to the hall for _____ .

The subject name _____ is usually shortened to Maths.

Art	Music	Assembly	History
Geography	Science	Mathematics	Design
Technology	Citizenship	English	Physical Education
French	German	Spanish	Religious Education
Drama	Information	Communication	Personal, Social, Health

Which words from the school timetable were not included in the sentences?

_____ _____ _____

_____ _____ _____

_____ _____

Opposites 1

This worksheet, together with sheets 3 and 4, features high frequency words and words that have been identified as appropriate for students at early secondary level.

 Focus on words

● Photocopy this page and the accompanying student worksheet. Discuss the focus words at the bottom of this page with the students. Ask them to write the words in the blank grid on their worksheet. You could dictate the words or, if appropriate, students could copy them from the set below.

● The completed grid on the worksheet, or the one below, could be laminated as a pocket reference card that students could refer to later.

● To analyse the words further, and if appropriate for your students, you could complete the following activities.

Segmenting the words into their phonemes

Explain to the students that they are going to segment some of the words into their separate sounds. Demonstrate with the word *beginning* by drawing lines between the graphemes that represent the separate phonemes: /b/e/g/i/nn/i/ng/. Now look at *business*. This is not an easy word to segment into phonemes as it includes a letter **i** that is not sounded; also, the letter **u** is making the phoneme /i/. You could represent it like this: /b/u/s/i/n/e/ss/. Ask the students to try segementing *disappear* and *jealous*. They may come up with different answers from each other but the important part of the activity is the process of hearing the separate sounds and observing how they are represented by graphemes.

Splitting the words into their syllables (syllabification)

For most students syllabification is much easier than segmenting. Explain that they are now going to split the words into 'chunks' of sound and give the example of *continuous: \con\tin\u\lous*. Can the students hear that the word can be split into four syllables? Discuss some single syllable words with the students such as *climb* and *health*. Ask the students if they think that *fierce* is a single syllable word. Point out that each syllable normally contains at least one vowel.

 Words in context

● When the students are ready ask them to complete the second activity on the worksheet.

audible	autumn	beginning	beneath
business	caught	climb	conscious
continuous	definite	disappear	fierce
health	imaginary	interesting	jealous
listening	lovely	modern	necessary

Opposites 1

Name _____

1 Write the focus words in the spaces on this grid.

For each of the words below find a word that means the opposite or nearly the opposite, from the words that you have written in the grid.

unconscious	_____	real	_____
horrible	_____	descend	_____
pleasure	_____	speaking	_____
silent	_____	broken	_____
dropped	_____	spring	_____
end	_____	boring	_____
illness	_____	unnecessary	_____
above	_____	appear	_____
unlikely	_____	old-fashioned	_____

Which words from the grid are not included above?

_____   _____

2 Write a sentence using as many of the words above as you can. How crazy can you make your sentence?

_____

_____

_____

Opposites 2

This worksheet, together with sheets 2 and 4, features high frequency words and words that have been identified as appropriate for students at early secondary level.

Teacher's Notes

Learning objective: Spelling high frequency words and their opposites

1 Focus on words

- Photocopy this page and the accompanying student worksheet. Discuss the focus words at the bottom of this page with the students. Ask them to write the words in the blank grid on their worksheet. You could dictate the words or, if appropriate, students could copy them from the set below.

- The completed grid on the worksheet, or the one below, could be laminated as a pocket reference card that students could refer to later.

- Discuss some of the words in more detail encouraging the students to notice particular features of some of the words e.g. the words *success* and *successful* contain double **c** and double **s**; the word *sincerely* has an **e** before the **l** but not after it; the /ae/ phoneme in *straight* is spelt with the grapheme /aigh/.

- To analyse the words further, and if appropriate for your students, you could complete the following activities.

  Segmenting the words into their phonemes
  Explain to the students that they are going to segment some of the words into their separate sounds. Demonstrate this with the word *secondary* by drawing lines between the graphemes that represent the separate phonemes: /s/e/c/o/n/d/ar/y/. Now look at *separate*: /s/e/p/a/r/a/te/. Here the final **e** works with the letter **a** to create the phoneme /ae/. In examining the rest of the words the students may come up with different answers from each other but the important part of the activity is the process of listening to the sounds and observing how they are represented by graphemes.

  Splitting the words into their syllables (syllabification)
  For most students syllabification is much easier than segmenting. Explain that they are now going to split the words into 'chunks' of sound and give the example of *permanent*: \per\ma\nent\. Can the students hear that the word can be split into three syllables? Now look at *fortunate* and ask the students to compare it to *fortunately*. Point out that each syllable normally contains at least one vowel but the final syllable of *fortunately* contains a letter **y** acting as a vowel.

2 Words in context

- When the students are ready ask them to complete the second activity on the worksheet.

nervous	original	permanent	receive
remember	safety	secondary	separate
sincerely	skilful	straight	strength
success	successful	surprise	tomorrow
unfortunately	fortunate	women	quiet

Opposites 2

Name _____

1 Write the focus words in the spaces on this grid.

For each of the words below find a word that means the opposite or nearly the opposite, from the words that you have written in the grid.

weakness _____

luckily _____

noisy _____

danger _____

unfortunate _____

give _____

brave _____

expected _____

primary _____

temporary _____

unoriginal _____

unskilled _____

unsuccessful _____

crooked _____

together _____

yesterday _____

forget _____

insincerely _____

men _____

failure _____

2 Write a sentence using as many of the words above as you can. How crazy can you make your sentence?

_____

_____

_____

_____

Opposites 3

This worksheet, together with sheets 2 and 4, features high frequency words and words that have been identified as appropriate for students at early secondary level.

Learning objective: Spelling high frequency words and their opposites

1 Focus on words

- Photocopy this page and the accompanying student worksheet. Discuss the focus words at the bottom of this page with the students. Ask them to write the words in the blank grid on their worksheet. You could dictate the words or, if appropriate, students could copy them from the set below.

- The completed grid on the worksheet, or the one below, could be laminated as a pocket reference card that students could refer to later.

- Discuss some of the words in more detail. The words *bought* and *brought* are often confused but by considering their opposites it is easier to make the distinction between them. Similarly, with the homophones *braking* and *breaking*.

- To analyse the words further, and if appropriate for your students, you could complete the following activities.

Segmenting the words into their phonemes
Explain to the students that they are going to segment some of the words into their separate sounds. Demonstrate with the word *beautiful* by drawing lines between the graphemes that represent the separate phonemes: /b/eau/t/i/f/u/l/. Ask the students to try some of the other words. They may come up with different answers from each other but the important part of the activity is in the process of hearing the separate sounds and observing how they are represented by graphemes.

Splitting the words into their syllables (syllabification)
For most students syllabification is much easier than segmenting. Explain that they are now going to split the words into 'chunks' of sound and give the example of *beautiful*: \beau\ti\ful\. Can the students hear that the word can be split into three syllables? You could also suggest that they break the word into 'false syllables', speaking each sound separately: \be\a\u\ti\ful\. Ask the students to try splitting some of the other words into syllables. Point out that each syllable normally contains at least one vowel.

2 Find the opposite

- When the students are ready ask them to complete the second activity on the worksheet.

aloud	bought	brought	braking
breaking	conscious	coarse	our
quietly	source	threw	whisper
beautiful	believe	conclusion	buried
column	creation	disappoint	enquire

Opposites 3

Name _____

1 Write the focus words in the spaces on this grid.

For each of the words below find a word that means the opposite or nearly the opposite, from the words that you have written in the grid.

shout	_____	dug up	_____
mending	_____	unconscious	_____
destruction	_____	sold	_____
their	_____	disbelieve	_____
accelerating	_____	please	_____
silently	_____	loudly	_____
answer	_____	caught	_____
start	_____	smooth	_____
row	_____	took	_____
mouth (of a river)	_____	ugly	_____

2 Write a sentence using as many as possible of the words above. How crazy can you make your sentence?

_____

_____

_____

Words ending with tion

1 Focus on words

- Photocopy this page and the accompanying student worksheet. Discuss the focus words at the bottom of this page with the students. Ask them to write the words in the blank grid on their worksheet. You could dictate the words or, if appropriate, students could copy them from the set below.

- The completed grid on the worksheet, or the one below, could be laminated as a pocket reference card that students could refer to later.

- To analyse the words further, and if appropriate for your students, you could complete the following activities.

  Segmenting the words into their phonemes

  Explain to the students that they are going to segment some of the words into their separate sounds. Present them with the problem of how to segment the letter string **tion** – is the letter **t** making the /sh/ sound? If so, are the letters **i** and **o** together saying /u/? Or, are the letters **t** and **i** together making the /sh/ sound? There are no simple answers to these questions but the discussion process enables the students to look closely at the letter string **tion**. They can then make their own choices about how to segment the words e.g. *reaction* could be segmented as /r/e/a/c/t/io/n/.

  Splitting the words into their syllables (syllabification)

  For most students syllabification is much easier than segmenting. Explain that they are now going to split the words into 'chunks' of sound and give the example of *accommodation: \ac\com\mo\da\tion*. Splitting the word in this way shows the importance of the double letter **c** and the double letter **m**.

2 Crossword puzzle

- When the students are ready ask them to complete the second activity on the worksheet – a crossword puzzle providing practice of the **tion** words they have been learning.

motion	action	reaction	portion
preparation	accommodation	concentration	participation
section	fraction	position	education
exploration	introduction	reflection	explanation
reservation	translation	infection	information

Words ending with tion

Name _____

1 Write the focus words in the spaces on this grid.

2 Twelve of the words from the grid are needed to complete the crossword.

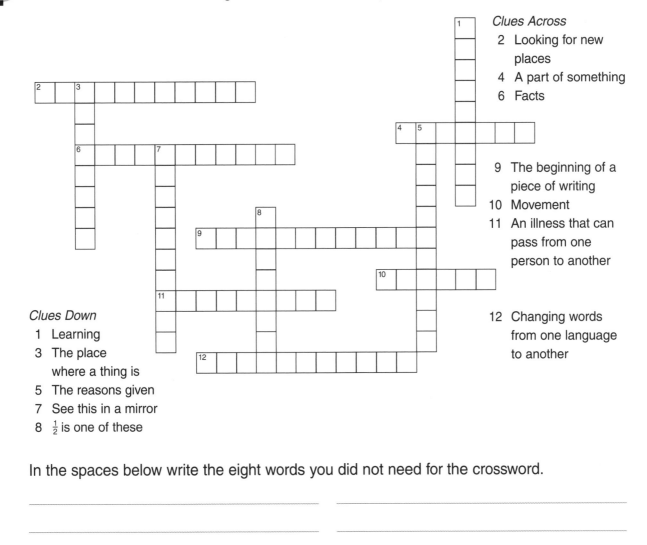

Clues Across

  2 Looking for new places

  4 A part of something

  6 Facts

  9 The beginning of a piece of writing

10 Movement

11 An illness that can pass from one person to another

12 Changing words from one language to another

Clues Down

  1 Learning

  3 The place where a thing is

  5 The reasons given

  7 See this in a mirror

  8 $\frac{1}{2}$ is one of these

In the spaces below write the eight words you did not need for the crossword.

_____   _____

_____   _____

_____   _____

_____   _____

Adding **ful**

Learning objective: Spelling words
ending in **ful** and **fully**

1 Focus on words

- Photocopy this page and the accompanying student worksheet. Discuss the focus words at the bottom of this page with the students. Ask them to write the words in the blank grid on their worksheet. You could dictate the words or, if appropriate, students could copy them from the set below.

- The completed grid on the worksheet, or the one below, could be laminated as a pocket reference card that students could refer to later.

- As one of the first activities you could ask the students to identify the odd-one-out: *fulfil*. Discuss whether this could be the combination of the two words *full* and *fill*. Encourage them to notice that both of these words have lost a letter **l**. What does the word *fulfil* mean? Can they use it in a sentence?

- To analyse the words further, and if appropriate for your students, you could complete the following activities.

  Segmenting the words into their phonemes
  Explain to the students that they are going to segment some of the words into their separate sounds. Demonstrate with the word *wonderful* by drawing lines between the graphemes that represent the separate phonemes: /w/o/n/d/er/f/u/l/. In completing this activity the students may come up with different answers from each other but the important part of the activity is the process of hearing the separate sounds and observing how they are represented by graphemes.

  Splitting the words into their syllables (syllabification)
  For most students syllabification is much easier than segmenting. Explain that they are now going to split the words into 'chunks' of sound and give the example of *plentifully*: \plen\ti\ful\ly\. Can the students hear that the word can be split into four syllables? Point out that each syllable normally contains at least one vowel and that the letter **y** is acting as a vowel in the last syllable.

2 Make new words

- When the students are ready, ask them to look at the second activity on the worksheet. Discuss the 'rules' with the students, ensuring that they understand how each rule works, then help them to apply the rules to the activity.

beautiful	wonderful	careful	fulfil
peaceful	hopeful	useful	cheerful
grateful	soulful	bowlful	armful
beautifully	carefully	peacefully	hopefully
wonderfully	gratefully	plentiful	plentifully

Adding **ful**

Name _____

1 Write the focus words in the spaces on this grid.

- We can add the suffix **ful** to words when we want to say *full of* e.g. if we want to say 'full of care' we can just write *careful*.

- But look at some of the words in the grid: *bowlful* does not mean 'full of bowl', it means that the bowl is full.

- Here are some rules about adding **ful**:

  For most words you just add **ful** e.g. care ⟶ careful

  For words that end in **y**, you take off the **y** and put **i** instead
  e.g. beauty ⟶ beautiful

2 Use the rules to add **ful** to the following words to make new words:

plenty ⟶ _____   cheer ⟶ _____

wonder ⟶ _____   beauty ⟶ _____

use ⟶ _____   hope ⟶ _____

Sometimes we want to add **full**. This time we keep the double letter **l**. Notice that for words that end in **y**, the **y** is replaced by **i**.

From the words below make new words that end in fully:

beauty ⟶ _____   grateful ⟶ _____

soul ⟶ _____   cheer ⟶ _____

peace ⟶ _____   plenty ⟶ _____

Words ending with **sion**

1 Focus on words

- Photocopy this page and the accompanying student worksheet. Discuss the focus words at the bottom of the page with the students. Ask them to write the words in the blank grid on their worksheet. You could dictate the words or, if appropriate, students could copy them from the set below.

- The completed grid on the worksheet, or the one below, could be laminated as a pocket reference card that students could refer to later.

- As part of your discussions you may like to ask the students to consider which words contain the letter **s** saying /zh/, such as *illusion*, and which words contain the letter **s** saying /sh/, such as *dimension*.

- To analyse the words further, and if appropriate for your students, you could complete the following activities.

  Segmenting the words into their phonemes
  Explain to the students that they are going to segment some of the words into their separate sounds. Present them with the problem of how to segment the letter string **sion**. Is the letter **s** making the /sh/ sound? If so, are the letters **i** and **o** together saying /u/? Or, are the letters **s** and **i** together making the /sh/ sound? There are no simple answers to these questions but the discussion process enables them to look closely at the letter string **sion**. They can make their own choices about how to segment the words e.g. *persuasion* could be segmented as /p/er/s/ua/s/io/n/.

  Splitting the words into their syllables (syllabification)
  For most students syllabification is much easier than segmenting. Explain that they are now going to split the words into 'chunks' of sound and give the example of *persuasion*: \per\sua\sion\ Can the students hear that the word can be split into three syllables?

2 Word puzzle

- When the students are ready ask them to complete the second activity on the worksheet, a puzzle providing practice of the *sion* words.

decision	persuasion	dimension	illusion
confusion	confession	revision	explosion
admission	percussion	expression	extension
television	transfusion	vision	mansion
conclusion	discussion	possession	collision

Words ending with **sion**

Name _____

1 Write the focus words in the spaces on this grid.

2 Follow the six clues to complete the puzzle. Each answer is one of the **sion** words from the grid. If your answers are correct a seventh word will appear in the shaded column. Write this word in the sentence below the puzzle.

Clues

1 Watch your favourite programme on this.

2 When two moving objects hit one another.

3 A very large house.

4 The cost of entry might be called an _____ fee.

5 A bomb might cause this.

6 A muddle.

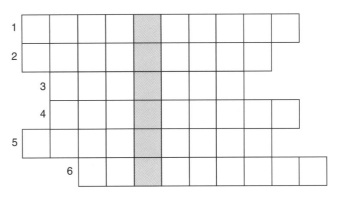

The sun shining on the clear blue sea was the most beautiful _____ he had ever seen.

Write the correct words in the following sentences.

The guilty person made a full _____ of his crimes.

The pupils had a long _____ about their holiday plans.

An _____ was built to add extra rooms to the house.

He was given a blood _____ after losing a lot of blood.

The drums and xylophone are _____ instruments.

A burglar stole many of their favourite _____.

After trying them several times, I reached the _____ that I didn't like sprouts.

It is important to do some careful _____ before a test.

Words containing ain

Learning objective:
Spelling words containing **ain**

1 Focus on words

- Photocopy this page and the accompanying student worksheet. Discuss the focus words at the bottom of this page with the students. Ask them to write the words in the blank grid on their worksheet. You could dictate the words or, if appropriate, students could copy them from the set below.

- The completed grid on the worksheet, or the one below, could be laminated as a pocket reference card that students could refer to later.

- Ask the students to identify the odd-one-out - *explanation* does not contain the letter string **ain** but is included because it is a derivative of the word *explain*.

- To analyse the words further, and if appropriate for your students, you could complete the following activities.

  Segmenting the words into their phonemes
  Explain to the students that they are going to segment some of the words into their separate sounds. Demonstrate with the word *complain* by drawing lines between the graphemes that represent the separate phonemes: /c/o/m/p/l/ai/n/. Ask the students to focus on the grapheme **ai** which is making the phoneme /ai/. Now look at *captain*: /c/a/p/t/ai/n/. This time, in most parts of the country, the grapheme **ai** is making the phoneme /i/. In the word *again*, in many parts of the country the grapheme **ai** is making the phoneme /e/.

  Splitting the words into their syllables (syllabification)
  For most students syllabification is much easier than segmenting. Explain that they are now going to split the words into 'chunks' of sound and give the example of *mountainous*: \moun\tain\ous\. Can the students hear that the word can be split into three syllables? Note that each syllable normally contains at least one vowel but in this case each syllable has two vowels.

2 Words in context

- When the students are ready ask them to complete the second activity on the worksheet, which provides practice in using the *ain* words within sentences.

curtain	again	complaint	fountain
Britain	mountain	terrain	certain
mountainous	explain	villain	maintain
captain	remain	bargain	complain
explanation	contain	entertain	obtain

Words containing ain

Name _____

1 Write the focus words in the spaces on this grid.

2 Write the missing words in these sentences.

"I don't normally _____ but today I have a very serious

_____ to make," said the miserable looking woman.

"I keep giving you an _____ . Do I have to _____

it all over again?" asked the maths teacher.

Much of _____ is relatively flat, especially East Anglia. However, in

Scotland the _____ is quite _____ .

The _____ of the Titanic was _____ that it was not

going to sink.

When the _____ came down at the end of the play there was loud

applause.

"Do you like my new phone?" she asked. "It was a real _____ because it

only cost fifty pounds."

Which words from the grid have not been used in the sentences?

_____   _____   _____

_____   _____   _____

_____   _____   _____

Occupations ending in **ist**, **cian**, **ian** and **yst**

1 Focus on words

- Photocopy this page and the accompanying student worksheet. Discuss the focus words at the bottom of this page with the students. Ask them to write the words in the blank grid on their worksheet. You could dictate the words or, if appropriate, students could copy them from the set below.

- The completed grid on the worksheet, or the one below, could be laminated as a pocket reference card that students could refer to later.

- To analyse the words further, and if more appropriate for your students, you could complete the following activities.

Segmenting the words into their phonemes

Explain to the students that they are going to segment some of the words into their separate sounds. Demonstrate with the word *optician* by drawing lines between the graphemes that represent the separate phonemes: /o/p/t/i/c/ia/n/. This process presents similar problems to the ones encountered with the letter strings **tion** or **sion** i.e. how do we segment the letter string **cian**? In completing this activity with the rest of the words, students may come up with different answers from each other but the important part of the activity is the process of hearing the separate sounds and observing how they are represented by graphemes. You may like to discuss with the students the fact that the letter string **cian** represents the phonemes /sh/, /u/ and /n/.

Splitting the words into their syllables (syllabification)

For most students syllabification is much easier than segmenting. Explain that they are now going to split the words into 'chunks' of sound and look again at the example of *optician*: \op\ti\cian\. Can the students hear that the word can be split into three syllables? Point out that each syllable normally contains at least one vowel.

2 Words in context

- When the students are ready ask them to complete the second activity on the worksheet, which provides practice of all the words.

dentist	magician	optician	dramatist
electrician	amphibian	technician	scientist
chemist	mathematician	politician	biologist
musician	beautician	pharmacist	physician
librarian	journalist	historian	analyst

Occupations ending in **ist**, **cian**, **ian** and **yst**

Name _____

1 Write the focus words in the spaces on this grid.

Nearly all of the words are names of occupations.
Which word is not the name of an occupation? _____

2 Complete the gaps in the words below and fill in the two missing clues.

Clue	Answer
This person does magic tricks	m __ g __ c __ __ n
This person works with numbers	m __ th __ __ at i c __ __ __
_____ _____	o p t i c i a n
The prime minister is one	p __ l __ t i __ __ __ __
This person makes music	m __ __ i c __ __ n
This person does technical things	__ __ __ __ n i c i a n
_____ _____	e l e c t r i c i a n
A person who helps you to look beautiful	b __ __ __ t __ c __ __ __

Words ending in ure

1 Focus on words

- Photocopy this page and the accompanying student worksheet. Discuss the focus words at the bottom of this page with the students. Ask them to write the words in the blank grid on their worksheet. You could dictate the words or, if appropriate, students could copy them from the set below.

- The completed grid on the worksheet, or the one below, could be laminated as a pocket reference card that students could refer to later.

- Discuss some of the words in more detail e.g. you could ask the students to identify the different sounds made by the letter string **ure** by listening to the words *nature* and *mature*. In *nature* the sound is short and makes the phoneme /er/, but in *mature* the sound is long and combines the phonemes /y/, /ue/ and /er/.

- To analyse the words further, and if appropriate for your students, you could complete the following activities.

  Segmenting the words into their phonemes
  Explain to the students that they are going to segment some of the words into their separate sounds. Demonstrate with the word *creature* by drawing lines between the graphemes that represent the separate phonemes: /c/r/ea/t/ure/. Ask the students what sound the letter **t** is making – is it making the phoneme /ch/?

  Splitting the words into their syllables (syllabification)
  For most students syllabification is much easier than segmenting. Explain that they are now going to split the words into 'chunks' of sound and look at the word *temperature*. In examining this word the students may notice that the second letter **e** is unsounded as we usually say this word in three syllables, not four: \tem\pera\ture\.

2 Meanings of words

- When the students are ready ask them to complete the second activity on the worksheet, which requires them to complete part words by referring to simple definitions.

nature	mature	creature	cure
structure	picture	literature	sure
pleasure	failure	leisure	measure
temperature	adventure	mixture	signature
agriculture	moisture	furniture	future

Words ending in ure

Name _____

1 Write the focus words in the spaces on this grid.

2 Complete the words below. Some clues have answers with missing letters. Some answers have no clues at all.

Clue	Answer
The natural world	n a __ __ __ __
Enjoyment	p l __ __ s __ __ __
Old or ripe	m a t __ __ __
Not succeeding	f a __ __ __ r e
_____	c r e a t u r e
A relaxing time	l __ __ s __ r __
To be made well	c __ __ __
You could do this using centimetres	m __ __ s __ __ e

Use some of the words to complete the sentences below.

She hoped the doctor would have a _____ for her illness.

I saw a strange looking _____ at the wildlife park.

She spent her _____ time reading or chatting to her friends.

Always _____ the window before buying new curtains.

Words containing sc

1 Focus on words

● Photocopy this page and the accompanying student worksheet. Discuss the focus words at the bottom of the page with the students. Ask them to write the words in the blank grid on their worksheet. You could dictate the words or, if appropriate, students could copy them from the set below.

● The completed grid on the worksheet, or the one below, could be laminated as a pocket reference card that students could refer to later.

● To analyse the words further, and if appropriate for your students, you could complete the following activities.

Segmenting the words into their phonemes
Explain to the students that they are going to segment some of the words into their separate sounds. Demonstrate with the word *discussion* by drawing lines between the graphemes that represent the separate phonemes: /d/i/s/c/u/ss/io/n/. You may like to ask students to compare this word to others that end with the letter string **tion**: *station, nation,* etc. All of these words end with the phonemes /sh/, /u/ and /n/.

Splitting the words into their syllables (syllabification)
For most students syllabification is much easier than segmenting. Explain that they are now going to split the words into 'chunks' of sound and give the example of *scientific*: \sci\en\ti\fic\. Can the students hear that the word can be split into four syllables?

2 Sort the words

● When the students are ready ask them to complete the second activity on the worksheet, which requires them to focus on the alternative sounds made by the grapheme *sc*.

science	disciple	discipline	discussion
muscle	scale	score	isosceles
scanner	scene	script	scenario
landscape	conscience	miscellaneous	scientific
disciplining	scenery	scientist	scan

Words containing sc

Name _____

1 Write the focus words in the spaces on this grid.

2 Look carefully at the words but listen carefully to them as well by saying them out loud.
In some of the words the two letters **s** and **c** combine to make the sound /s/.
In the others, the two letters make the two sounds /s/ and /k/.

Sort the words into two sets: those that have just the sound /s/ and those that have both sounds /s/ and /k/. The first two have been done for you.

/s/ sound	/s/ and /k/ sounds
science	scale

Write a sentence using as many **sc** words as possible.

_____

_____

_____

Words ending in tion

1 Focus on words

● Photocopy this page and the accompanying student worksheet. Discuss the focus words at the bottom of this page with the students. All these words can be found in the lists of suggested words for the early part of secondary education and they are all relevant to particular subject areas. Ask the students to write the words in the blank grid on their worksheet. You could dictate the words or, if appropriate, students could copy them from the set below.

● The completed grid on the worksheet, or the one below, could be laminated as a pocket reference card that students could refer to later.

● To analyse the words further, and if appropriate for your students, you could complete the following activities.

Segmenting the words into their phonemes
Explain to the students that they are going to segment some of the words into their separate sounds. Remind them of the problem of how to segment the letter string **tion** – is the letter **t** making the /sh/ sound? If so, are the letters **i** and **o** together saying /u/? Or, are the letters **t** and **i** together making the /sh/ sound? There are no simple answers to these questions but the process of discussing them encourages the student to look closely at the letter string **tion**. They can make their own decisions about how to segment the words e.g. *evaporation* could be segmented as /e/v/a/p/or/a/t/io/n/.

Splitting the words into their syllables (syllabification)
For most students syllabification is much easier than segmenting. Explain that they are now going to split the words into 'chunks' of sound and give the example *personification*: \per\son\if\i\ca\tion\. Again, the word could be split in slightly different ways but the process is the same and encourages the students to look carefully at the word and how it is constructed.

2 Sorting words

● When the students are ready ask them to complete the second activity on the worksheet. Help them to sort the words according to school subjects. Some words may be relevant to more than one subject area but the important part of the process is the reading and re-reading of the words, together with the speaking, listening and decision-making. All of these encourage the students to look closely at the words.

evaporation	conjunction	pollution	constitution
revolution	proportion	friction	fiction
colonisation	connection	equation	creation
syncopation	celebration	resolution	specification
composition	personification	evaluation	production

Words ending in tion

Name _____

1 Write the focus words in the spaces on this grid.

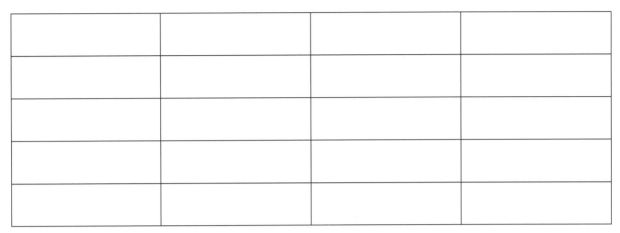

2 Try to sort the focus words into the boxes below, according to the subjects in which you might use them. Some boxes may have no suitable words and some words may belong in more than one box.

Music	**History**	**Geography**	**Science**

Mathematics	**DT**	**Drama**	**ICT**

Words ending in al

Learning objective: Understanding what a suffix is and spelling words ending in **al**

1 Focus on words

- Photocopy this page and the accompanying student worksheet. Discuss the focus words at the bottom of this page with the students. Ask them to write the words in the blank grid on their worksheet. You could dictate the words or, if appropriate, students could copy them from the set below.

- The completed grid on the worksheet, or the one below, could be laminated as a pocket reference card that students could refer to later.

- Discuss the idea of suffixes with the students. Explain that a suffix is a word ending that can be added to a word to change its meaning. Although all of the focus words have the **al** ending, it is not always a suffix to a modern word e.g. if we remove the **al** from the word *funeral* we find 'funer', which is not a word in itself. However, if we remove the **al** from the word *regional* we find 'region', which is a word. The activity on the worksheet helps the students with this concept. (Note that if a root word ends with a letter **e**, that letter needs to be removed before the suffix **al** is added and if a root word ends with a letter **y**, that letter needs to be replaced with a letter **i**.) Some root words have **ical** added as the suffix: theatre, theatrical; Bible, biblical.

- To analyse the words further, and if appropriate for your students, you could complete the following activities.

  Segmenting the words into their phonemes
  Explain to the students that they are going to segment some of the words into their separate sounds. Demonstrate with the word *mineral* by drawing lines between the graphemes that represent the separate phonemes: /m/i/n/er/a/l/. In completing the activity students may come up with different answers from each other but the important part of the activity is the process of learning the separate sounds and observing how they are represented by graphemes.

  Splitting the words into their syllables (syllabification)
  For most students syllabification is much easier than segmenting. Explain that they are now going to split the words into 'chunks' of sound and give the example of *theatrical: \the\at\ri\cal*. Can the students hear that the word can be split into four syllables? Point out that each syllable normally contains at least one vowel.

2 Rules for suffixes

- Once the students have completed the grid support them in working through the remaining activities on the sheet. They will need guidance in looking very closely at the words and the 'rules' regarding adding the suffix.

mineral	rehearsal	theatrical	industrial
plural	international	regional	material
rural	agricultural	cathedral	chronological
funeral	alphabetical	economical	equilateral
quadrilateral	symmetrical	approval	biblical

Words ending in al

Name _____

1 Write the focus words in the spaces on this grid.

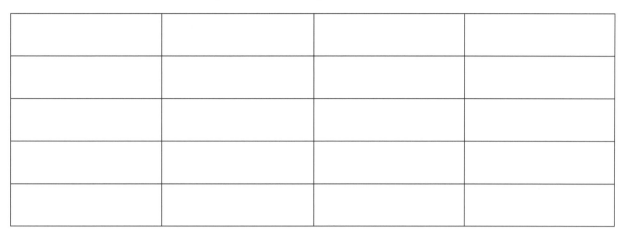

- Some of the **al** words are made from shorter words
  e.g. instrument ⟶ instrumental

  An ending added to a word to change its meaning is called a suffix. **al** is a suffix that can be added to the word *instrument*.

- If the root word ends with a letter **e**, you have to remove that letter **e** before adding the suffix **al** e.g. rehearse ⟶ rehearsal

- If the root word ends with a letter **y**, you have to remove that letter **y** and replace it with an **i** before adding the suffix **al**.

- Some of the shorter words need to have the suffix **ical** added to them.

Add the suffix **al** or **ical** to the following words:

region _____   Bible _____

economic _____   symmetry _____

theatre _____   chronology _____

rehearse _____   industry _____

alphabet _____

2 Look again at the words in the grid. Which ones do not make a shorter word if the suffixes **al** or **ical** are removed?

_____ _____ _____

_____ _____ _____

_____ _____ _____

Words ending in **ally**

Teacher's Notes

Learning objective: Understanding what a suffix is and spelling words ending in **ally.** Sorting words into alphabetical order.

1 Focus on words

- Photocopy this page and the accompanying student worksheet. Discuss the focus words at the bottom of this page with the students. Ask them to write the words in the blank grid on their worksheet. You could dictate the words or, if appropriate, students could copy them from the set below.

- The completed grid on the worksheet, or the one below, could be laminated as a pocket reference card that students could refer to later.

- Encourage the students to notice that all the focus words ending in **ally** have simply had the suffix **ly** added to the shorter words that end with **al**. This provides a good illustration of the fact that the suffix **ly** is normally added to a complete word. You could remind the students that adding **ly** to the word *love* gives the spelling *lovely* not *lovly*. More examples of this can be found on Worksheet 16. Note that in some cases a root word has had two suffixes added e.g. nation – national – nationally. Ask the students which of the words follow this pattern.

- To analyse the words further, and if appropriate for your students, you could complete the following activities.

  Segmenting the words into their phonemes
  Explain to the students that they are going to segment some of the words into their separate sounds. Demonstrate with the word *politically* by drawing lines between the graphemes that represent the separate phonemes: /p/o/l/i/t/i/c/a/ll/y/. In completing this activity with the rest of the words, the students may come up with different answers from each other but the important part of the activity is the process of hearing the separate sounds and observing how they are represented by graphemes.

  Splitting the words into their syllables (syllabification)
  For most students syllabification is much easier than segmenting. Explain that they are now going to split the words into 'chunks' of sound and give the example again of *politically:* \pol\it\ic\al\ly\. Can the students hear that the word can be split into five syllables?

2 Words in context

- When the students are ready ask them to complete the second activity on the worksheet, sorting the words into alphabetical order then writing a sentence containing as many words as possible that end with **ally**.

actual	natural	political	national
horizontal	vertical	personal	emotional
moral	special	actually	naturally
politically	nationally	horizontally	vertically
personally	emotionally	morally	specially

Words ending in **ally**

Name _____

1 Write the focus words in the spaces on this grid.

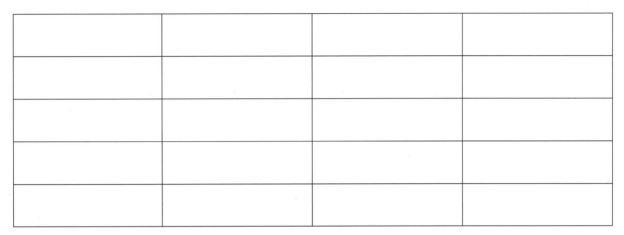

2 Look at the words *natural* and *naturally*. If we want to write them in alphabetical order we would write *natural* first – it contains exactly the same letters as the first seven letters of *naturally* but it is shorter so we write it first.

Try to write the twenty focus words in alphabetical order.

_____   _____
_____   _____
_____   _____
_____   _____
_____   _____
_____   _____
_____   _____
_____   _____
_____   _____
_____   _____

Write a sentence containing as many **ally** words as possible.

_____
_____
_____

More words ending in tion

1 Focus on words

● Photocopy this page and the accompanying student worksheet. Discuss the focus words at the bottom of the page with the students. Ask them to write the words in the blank grid on their worksheet. You could dictate the words or, if appropriate, students could copy them from the set below. All of these focus words can be found in the lists of suggested words for the early part of secondary education and they are all relevant to particular subject areas.

● The completed grid on the worksheet, or the one below, could be laminated as a pocket reference card that students could refer to later.

● To analyse the words further, and if appropriate for your students, you could complete the following activities.

Segmenting the words into their phonemes
Explain to the students that they are going to segment some of the words into their separate sounds. Remind them of the problem of how to segment the letter string **tion** – is the letter **t** making the /sh/ sound? If so, are the letters **i** and **o** together saying /u/? Or, are the letters **t** and **i** together making the /sh/ sound? There are no simple answers to these questions but the process of discussing them encourages the student to look closely at the letter string **tion**. Students can make their own decisions about how to segment the words e.g. *situation* could be segmented as /s/i/t/u/a/t/io/n/.

Splitting the words into their syllables (syllabification)
For most students syllabification is much easier than segmenting. Explain that they are now going to split the words into 'chunks' of sound and give the example of *transportation: \trans\por\ta\tion*. Again, the word could be split in slightly different ways but the process is the same and encourages the students to look carefully at the word and how it is constructed.

2 Sorting words

● When the students are ready ask them to complete the second activity on the worksheet. Help the students to sort the words according to school subjects. Some words may be relevant to more than one subject area but the important part of the process is the reading and re-reading of the words, together with the speaking, listening and decision-making. All of these encourage the students to look closely at the words.

situation	transportation	civilisation	function
respiration	alliteration	reproduction	exclamation
nutrition	subtraction	communication	digestion
circulation	addition	addiction	collection
exhibition	solution	emotion	condensation

More words ending in **tion**

Name _____

1 Write the focus words in the spaces on this grid.

2 Try to sort the words into the boxes below, according to the subjects in which you might use them. Some boxes may have no suitable words and some words may belong in more than one box.

Art	Music	History	Geography

Science	Mathematics	PSHE	English

Adding and removing the **ly** ending

Learning objective: Understanding what a suffix is and spelling words ending in **ly**

1 Focus on words

- Photocopy this page and the accompanying student worksheet. Discuss the focus words at the bottom of the page with the students. Ask them to write the words in the blank grid on their worksheet. You could dictate the words or, if appropriate, students could copy them from the set below.

- The completed grid on the worksheet, or the one below, could be laminated as a pocket reference card that students could refer to later.

- Explain to the students that all the words are made from shorter words and that the suffix **ly** has been added to them to make them into adverbs or adjectives. In most cases the **ly** has simply been added. Ask the students to identify which two words have needed changes before adding the **ly**.

- To analyse the words further, and if appropriate for your students, you could complete the following activities.

  Segmenting the words into their phonemes
  Explain to the students that they are going to segment some of the words into their separate sounds and give the example of *daily* by drawing lines between the graphemes that represent the separate phonemes: /d/ai/l/y/. In completing the activity with the rest of the words, students may come up with different answers from each other but the important part of the activity is in the process of hearing the separate sounds and observing how they are represented by graphemes.

  Splitting the words into their syllables (syllabification)
  For most students syllabification is much easier than segmenting. Explain that they are now going to split the words into 'chunks' of sound and give the example of *unfortunately:* \un\for\tu\nate\ly\. Can the students hear that the word can be split into five syllables?

2 Words in context

- When the students are ready ask them to complete the second activity on the worksheet, which requires them to reverse the process of adding suffixes and therefore encourages them to look closely at the rule again. The final activity provides an opportunity for the students to consider two homophones and to create different sentences for them.

fortunately	unfortunately	appropriately	lonely
lovely	approximately	carefully	weekly
weakly	monthly	annually	daily
hourly	firstly	secondly	thirdly
fourthly	fifthly	strongly	happily

Adding and removing the ly ending

Name _____

1 Write the focus words in the spaces on this grid.

2 Remove the suffix **ly** from all of the words to create shorter words. Most of the words are easy to do but look out for the two that need special attention.

_____ _____

_____ _____

_____ _____

_____ _____

_____ _____

_____ _____

_____ _____

_____ _____

_____ _____

The words **weekly** and **weakly** are homophones. They sound the same but they are spelt differently and they mean different things. Write two sentences, one using the word **weekly** and one using the word **weakly**.

_____

_____

_____

_____

Words where **y** behaves like a vowel

Teacher's Notes

Learning objective: Spelling words where **y** behaves like a vowel

1 Focus on words

● Photocopy this page and the accompanying student worksheet. Discuss the focus words at the bottom of this page with the students. Ask them to write the words in the blank grid on their worksheet. You could dictate the words or, if appropriate, students could copy them from the set below.

● The completed grid on the worksheet, or the one below, could be laminated as a pocket reference card that students could refer to later.

● To analyse the words further, and if appropriate for your students, you could complete the following activities.

Segmenting the words into their phonemes

Explain to the students that they are going to segment some of the words into their separate sounds. Demonstrate with the word *February* by drawing lines between the graphemes that represent the separate phonemes: /F/e/b/r/u/a/r/y/. Discuss the fact that here the letter **y** is making the phoneme /ee/. Ask the students to try some of the other words.

Splitting the words into their syllables (syllabification)

For most students syllabification is much easier than segmenting. Explain that they are now going to split the words into 'chunks' of sound and look again at *February* as it is so often spelt incorrectly: \Feb\ru\a\ry\. Can the students hear that the word can be split into four syllables? Can they hear the sound of the first letter **r**?

2 Sort the words

● When the students are ready ask them to complete the second activity on the worksheet. Help them to sort the words according to the sound made by the letter **y**.

analyse	analysis	February	acrylic
imagery	authority	dynasty	megabyte
dictionary	photocopy	dynamics	rhythm
activity	mobility	reality	symbol
oxygen	synagogue	cycle	laboratory

Words where **y** behaves like a vowel

Name _____

1 Write the focus words in the spaces on this grid.

2 Each of the focus words includes a letter **y** that is acting as a vowel. However, in some words it makes different vowel sounds from those it makes in others e.g.

In the word **February**, the letter **y** makes the sound /ee/ - this is called the long **e** sound.

In the word **analyse**, the letter **y** makes the sound /ie/ - this is called the long **i** sound.

In the word **analysis**, the letter **y** makes the sound /i/ - this is called the short **i** sound.

Sort the focus words into three lists.

/ee/	/ie/	/i/
_____	_____	_____
_____	_____	_____
_____	_____	_____
_____	_____	_____
_____	_____	_____
_____	_____	_____
_____	_____	_____
_____	_____	_____
_____	_____	_____

Which word appeared in two lists? _____

More words where **y** behaves like a vowel

1 Focus on words

- Photocopy this page and the accompanying student worksheet. Discuss the focus words at the bottom of this page with the students. Ask them to write the words in the blank grid on their worksheet. You could dictate the words or, if appropriate, students could copy them from the set below.

- The completed grid on the worksheet, or the one below, could be laminated as a pocket reference card that students could refer to later.

- To analyse the words further, and if appropriate for your students, you could complete the following activities.

  Segmenting the words into their phonemes

  Explain to the students that they are going to segment some of the words into their separate sounds. Demonstrate with the word *memory* by drawing lines between the graphemes that represent the separate phonemes: /m/e/m/or/y/. Discuss the fact that here the letter **y** is making the phoneme /ee/. Notice also that each letter is making a separate phoneme.

  Splitting the words into their syllables (syllabification)

  For most students syllabification is much easier than segmenting. Explain that they are now going to split the words into 'chunks' of sound and give the example of *harmony*: \har\mon\y\. Can the students hear that the word can be split into three syllables?

2 Sort the words

- When the students are ready ask them to complete the second activity on the worksheet. Help them to sort the words according to the sound made by the letter **y**. As an extra activity it would also be helpful to look closely at the word *encyclopaedia* where the grapheme **ae** is creating the phoneme /ee/.

diary	energy	strategy	hygiene
myth	country	county	justify
encyclopaedia	lyric	harmony	memory
synchronise	agility	qualify	stereotype
surely	polyester	synonym	vocabulary

44

More words where **y** behaves like a vowel

Name _____

1 Write the focus words in the spaces on this grid.

2 Each of the focus words includes a letter **y** that is acting as a vowel. However, in some words it makes different vowel sounds to those it makes in others e.g.

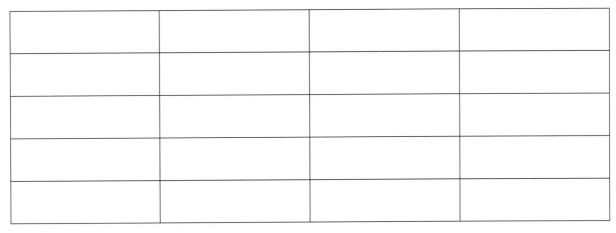

In the word **energy**, the letter **y** makes the sound /ee/ - the long **e** sound.

In the word **hygiene**, the letter **y** makes the sound /ie/ - the long **i** sound.

In the word **myth**, the letter **y** makes the sound /i/ - the short **i** sound.

Sort the focus words into three lists.

/ee/	/ie/	/i/
_____	_____	_____
_____	_____	_____
_____	_____	_____
_____	_____	_____
_____	_____	_____
_____	_____	_____
_____	_____	_____
_____	_____	_____

In which of the words does the letter **y** appear twice making the same sound? _____

Even more words where y behaves like a vowel

Learning objective: Spelling more words where **y** behaves like a vowel

1 Focus on words

- Photocopy this page and the accompanying student worksheet. Discuss the focus words at the bottom of this page with the students. Ask them to write the words in the blank grid on their worksheet. You could dictate the words or, if appropriate, students could copy them from the set below.

- The completed grid on the worksheet, or the one below, could be laminated as a pocket reference card that students could refer to later.

- To analyse the words further, and if appropriate for your students, you could complete the following activities.

  Segmenting the words into their phonemes

  Explain to the students that they are going to segment some of the words into their separate sounds. Demonstrate with the word *copyright* by drawing lines between the graphemes that represent the separate phonemes: */c/o/p/y/r/igh/t/*. Discuss the fact that here the letter **y** is making the phoneme */ee/*. Notice also that the grapheme **igh** is making the phoneme */ie/*.

  Splitting the words into their syllables (syllabification)

  For most students syllabification is much easier than segmenting. Explain that they are now going to split the words into 'chunks' of sound and give the example of *gymnastics: \gym\nas\tics*. Can the students hear that the word can be split into three syllables?

2 Sort the words

- When the students are ready ask them to complete the second activity on the worksheet. Help them to sort the words according to the sound made by the letter **y**. Many of the words are considered as core vocabulary in certain school subjects. As an extension activity you could ask the students to identify under which subject heading each word could belong, much as they did on Worksheets 12 and 15.

estuary	binary	byte	anthology
copyright	fantasy	multiply	gym
glossary	symmetry	melody	gymnastics
syncopation	ability	injury	generosity
ceremony	hymn	gigabyte	geology

Even more words where **y** behaves like a vowel

Name _____

1 Write the focus words in the spaces on this grid.

2 Each of the focus words includes a letter **y** that is acting as a vowel. However, in some words it makes different vowel sounds from those it makes in others e.g.

In the word **estuary**, the letter **y** makes the sound /ee/ - the long **e** sound.

In the word **multiply**, the letter **y** makes the sound /ie/ - the long **i** sound.

In the word **gym**, the letter **y** makes the sound /i/ - the short **i** sound.

Sort the focus words into three lists.

/ee/   **/ie/**

_____   _____   _____

_____   _____   _____

_____   _____   _____

_____   _____   **/i/**

_____   _____   _____

_____   _____   _____

_____   _____

                                    _____

Try to write a sentence that includes three words each with a different **y** sound.

_____

_____

Words ending in ism

1 Focus on words

- Photocopy this page and the accompanying student worksheet. Discuss the focus words at the bottom of this page with the students. Ask them to write the words in the blank grid on their worksheet. You could dictate the words or, if appropriate, students could copy them from the set below.

- The completed grid on the worksheet, or the one below, could be laminated as a pocket reference card that students could refer to later.

- The students may need considerable help with the meaning of some of the words: it may be helpful to consider the words that they are likely to know and understand already e.g. they will probably know that a person who shows racism is a racist.

- Discuss some of the words in more detail – a worthwhile activity again is to ask the students which of the words could be linked to specific school subjects e.g. Sikhism, Hinduism and Buddhism are linked to RE; organism is linked to science. Several of the words can be linked to art. Sexism and racism may be discussed in Citizenship or PSHE.

- To analyse the words further, and if appropriate for your students, you could complete the following activities.

  Segmenting the words into their phonemes
  Explain to the students that they are going to segment some of the words into their separate sounds. Demonstrate with the word *organism* by drawing lines between the graphemes that represent the separate phonemes: /or/g/a/n/i/s/m/. In completing this activity with the rest of the words, the students may come up with different answers from each other but the important part of the activity is the process of hearing the separate sounds and observing how they are represented by graphemes.

  Splitting the words into their syllables (syllabification)
  For most students syllabification is much easier than segmenting. Explain that they are now going to split the words into 'chunks' of sound and give the example of *imperialism: \im\pe\ri\al\is\m*. Can the students hear that the word can be split into six syllables?

2 Word families

- When the students are ready ask them to complete the second activity on the worksheet, which encourages them to recognize word families.

idealism	organism	Sikhism	imperialism
sexism	Buddhism	impressionism	tourism
Hinduism	expressionism	extremism	romanticism
symbolism	mannerism	racism	modernism

Words containing ism

Name _____

1 Write the focus words in the spaces on this grid.

2 Many of the focus words are related to other words e.g. we could say that someone who is an **idealist** would show **idealism**.

For each of the words, try to write at least one related word. For some words you may be able to think of more.

idealism	**organism**	**Sikhism**	**imperialism**

sexism	**Buddhism**	**impressionism**	**tourism**

Hinduism	**expressionism**	**extremism**	**romanticism**

symbolism	**mannerism**	**racism**	**modernism**

Words with silent letters

1 Focus on words

- Photocopy this page and the accompanying student worksheet. Discuss the focus words at the bottom of this page with the students. Ask them to write the words in the blank grid on their worksheet. You could dictate the words or, if appropriate, students could copy them from the set below.

- The completed grid on the worksheet, or the one below, could be laminated as a pocket reference card that students could refer to later.

- Talk to the students about silent letters. Can they identify which is the silent letter in each word? Have some of the words got more than one silent letter? In some of the words there are graphemes that have been covered on previous worksheets e.g. the **sc** in the word *scene*. Ask the students whether they think that the letter **c** is a silent letter in *scene* in the same way that the letter **p** is a silent letter in the word *psalm*. Remind the students of the need to write a letter **u** after the letter **q**, as they can see in the word *queue*.

- To analyse the words further, and if appropriate for your students, you could complete the following activities.
  Segmenting the words into their phonemes
  Explain to the students that they are going to segment some of the words into their separate sounds. Demonstrate with the word *chocolate* by drawing lines between the graphemes that represent the separate phonemes: /ch/o/c/o/l/a/t/e/. Discuss the following issues with the students: Is this the correct split? Should the second letter **o** be separated out at all as we can't hear it when we say the word? Should the phoneme /ae/ be represented differently?
  Splitting the words into their syllables (syllabification)
  For most students this valuable activity is much easier and works very successfully with all of the words except *chocolate* and *people*. The question again is what happens to that letter **o** in each of these two words? The discussion of this should highlight that the letter is 'silent' and should help the students to learn the spelling of the words. The other words are more straightforward e.g. \rhom\bus\, \stom\ach\.

2 Words in context

- When the students are ready ask them to complete the second activity on the worksheet, which encourages them to practise the focus words by writing them within sentences.

column	people	autumn	chocolate
design	rhyme	guard	psalm
playwright	rhombus	climber	whistle
marriage	queue	stomach	knife
hymn	castle	Buddhist	knowledge

Words with silent letters

Name _____

1 Write the focus words in the spaces on this grid.

Look carefully at each of the words and decide which letters are silent. Choose seven of the words. Write them down and then, for each one, write the silent letter or letters.

column   rhombus   hymn   climber
design   marriage   stomach
Buddhist   rhyme
people   knowledge
knife   psalm   whistle
guard   castle
chocolate   playwright   queue

_____ _____
_____ _____
_____ _____
_____ _____
_____ _____
_____ _____
_____ _____

2 Write the missing words in these sentences.

Bonfire night takes place in the _____ .

When he first wrote the play the _____ tried to make the words

_____ .

The police had to _____ the royal visitor.

The _____ starts with the wedding ceremony.

Write your own sentence using at least two of the words from the grid.

_____

_____

_____

Words containing ence or ance

Learning objective: Spelling words ending in **ence** or **ance**

1 Focus on words

- Photocopy this page and the accompanying student worksheet. Discuss the focus words at the bottom of this page with the students. Ask them to write the words in the blank grid on their worksheet. You could dictate the words or, if appropriate, students could copy them from the set below.

- The completed grid on the worksheet, or the one below, could be laminated as a pocket reference card that students could refer to later.

- Ask the students if they think that there is an odd-one-out. Hopefully they will identify the word *suspense*, as its closing phoneme */s/* is written with the grapheme **se** rather than the grapheme **ce**. They may also identify the words *dependency* and *frequency* as being different from the other words as they end with letter **y** rather than letter **e**. Remind the students of the need to write a letter **u** after the letter **q**, as they can see in the word *sequence*.

- To analyse the words further, and if appropriate for your students, you could complete the following activities.
  Segmenting the words into their phonemes
  Explain to the students that they are going to segment some of the words into their separate sounds. Demonstrate with the word *distance* by drawing lines between the graphemes that represent the separate phonemes: */d/i/s/t/a/n/ce/*. In completing the activity with the rest of the words, students may come up with different answers from each other but the important part of the activity is in the process of hearing the separate sounds and observing how they are represented by graphemes.
  Splitting the words into their syllables (syllabification)
  For most students syllabification is much easier than segmenting. Explain that they are now going to split the words into 'chunks' of sound and give the example *performance: \per\for\mance*.

2 Sort the words

- When the students are ready ask them to complete the second activity on the worksheet, which encourages them to look closely at the words and to identify the different word endings.

audience	instance	consequence	performance
sequence	defence	independence	relevance
irrelevance	romance	circumference	preference
dependency	frequency	pence	suspense
offence	fence	distance	conscience

Words containing ence or ance

Name _____

1 Write the focus words in the spaces on this grid.

2 Which words end with **ence**?

_____

_____

_____

_____

_____

_____

_____

_____

_____

Which words end with **ance**?

_____

_____

_____

_____

_____

Which words end with **ency**?

_____

_____

Which words end with **ense**?

_____

Write a sentence including as many of the focus words as you can.

_____

_____

_____

Words ending in ent

1 Focus on words

- Photocopy this page and the accompanying student worksheet. Discuss the focus words at the bottom of this page with the students. Ask them to write the words in the blank grid on their worksheet. You could dictate the words or, if appropriate, students could copy them from the set below.

- The completed grid on the worksheet, or the one below, could be laminated as a pocket reference card that students could refer to later.

- To analyse the words further, and if appropriate for your students, you could complete the following activities.

  Segmenting the words into their phonemes

  Explain to the students that they are going to segment some of the words into their separate sounds. Demonstrate with the word *content* by drawing lines between the graphemes that represent the separate phonemes: /c/o/n/t/e/n/t/. Like many of the words on this worksheet, each letter represents a phoneme. Compare this to the words *employment* and *parliament*. Discuss particularly the phoneme represented by the grapheme **ia** in *parliament*.

  Splitting the words into their syllables (syllabification)

  For most students syllabification is much easier than segmenting. Explain that they are now going to split the words into 'chunks' of sound and give the example of *environment*: \en\vi\ron\ment\. Point out that usually each syllable needs at least one vowel.

2 Alphabetical order

- When the students are ready ask them to complete the second activity on the worksheet. Help the students to identify the words that do not end in **ment**: *independent, permanent, component, content, nutrient*. Pay particular attention to *independent* as many students are tempted to end this word with **ant** instead of **ent**.

argument	environment	advertisement	government
independent	commandment	assessment	permanent
employment	parliament	achievement	commitment
development	component	settlement	content
encouragement	element	movement	nutrient

Words ending in ent

Name _____

1 Write the focus words in the spaces on this grid.

2 Look at the words carefully. Most of them end with **ment**. Which ones do not?

_____   _____   _____

_____   _____   _____

Time yourself. See how quickly you can organise all the words into alphabetical order on the lines below.

1 _____   11 _____

2 _____   12 _____

3 _____   13 _____

4 _____   14 _____

5 _____   15 _____

6 _____   16 _____

7 _____   17 _____

8 _____   18 _____

9 _____   19 _____

10 _____   20 _____

Write one sentence that includes the words *government* and *parliament*.

_____

_____

Words ending in ant

Teacher's Notes

Learning objective: Spelling words ending in **ant**

1 Focus on words

- Photocopy this page and the accompanying student worksheet. Discuss the focus words at the bottom of this page with the students. The **ent** ending featured on Worksheet 23 is more common than the **ant** ending but it is often difficult for students to decide which one is correct when they are attempting to spell a particular word. There are some clues that can help e.g. the ending **ant** often means 'one who' as in the word assistant meaning 'one who assists', or an occupant meaning 'one who occupies'. Many of the **ant** words are adjectives describing someone's particular attribute. A good way to remember this is to consider that the 'someone' is an ant: the extravagant ant, the pleasant ant, the reluctant ant, etc.

- The completed grid on the worksheet, or the one below, could be laminated as a pocket reference card that students could refer to later.

- Ask the students to write the words in the blank grid on their worksheet. You could dictate the words or, if appropriate, students could copy them from the set below.

- To analyse the words further, and if appropriate for your students, you could complete the following activities.

  Segmenting the words into their phonemes
  Explain to the students that they are going to segment some of the words into their separate sounds. Demonstrate with the word *pleasant* by drawing lines between the graphemes that represent the separate phonemes: /p/l/ea/s/a/n/t/. In completing the activity with the rest of the words, students may come up with different answers from each other but the important part of the activity is in the process of hearing the separate sounds and observing how they are represented by graphemes.

  Splitting the words into their syllables (syllabification)
  For most students syllabification is much easier than segmenting. Explain that they are now going to split the words into 'chunks' of sound and give the example of *extravagant: \ex\tra\va\gant*. Can the students hear that the word can be split into four syllables? Can they hear the vowel phoneme /a/ three times?

2 Alphabetical order

- When the students are ready ask them to complete the second activity on the worksheet where they are asked to time themselves in organizing the words into alphabetical order. This is an activity that many students will find difficult and they may need considerable help.

accountant	extravagant	brilliant	instant
assistant	constant	occupant	servant
pleasant	reluctant	important	attendant
distant	ignorant	inhabitant	pendant
stagnant	vacant	protestant	repentant

Words ending in ant

Name _____

1 Write the focus words in the spaces on this grid.

2 Time yourself. See how quickly you can organise all the words into alphabetical order on the lines below.

1 _____   11 _____

2 _____   12 _____

3 _____   13 _____

4 _____   14 _____

5 _____   15 _____

6 _____   16 _____

7 _____   17 _____

8 _____   18 _____

9 _____   19 _____

10 _____   20 _____

Write one sentence that includes the words *extravagant* and *accountant*.

_____

_____

_____

Adding endings to two-syllable words

Learning objective: To recognise rules for adding common endings to words

1 Focus on words

Photocopy this page and the accompanying student worksheet. Discuss the focus words at the bottom of this page with the students. Ask them to write the words in the blank grid on their worksheet. You could dictate the words or, if appropriate, students could copy them from the set below.

Students will be familiar with rules regarding adding endings to one-syllable words e.g. if a word ends with a vowel then a consonant, we double the consonant so *stop* becomes *stopped* but if a word already ends with a double consonant we simply add the ending so *rock* becomes *rocking*. If a word ends with a consonant then **e** we remove the **e** so *bite* becomes *biting*. With two-syllable words, the general rule is to decide which syllable is being stressed. If the first syllable is stressed we just add the ending e.g. *happen – happening*. If the second syllable is stressed we double the consonant then add the ending e.g. *begin – beginning*. Notice that we have included *benefit* although it is a three-syllable word but it follows the same rules as the first syllable is stressed e.g. *benefit – benefited*.

The completed grid on the worksheet, or the one below, could be laminated as a pocket reference card that students could refer to later.

To analyse the words further, and if appropriate for your students, you could complete the following activities.

Segmenting the words into their phonemes
Explain to the students that they are going to segment some of the words into their separate sounds. Demonstrate with the word *visiting* by drawing lines between the graphemes that represent the separate phonemes: /v/i/s/i/t/i/ng/. In completing the activity the students may come up with different answers from each other but the important part of the activity is the process of hearing the separate sounds and observing how they are represented by graphemes.

Splitting the words into their syllables (syllabification)
With each word that we are considering here we need to decide not only how many syllables the word has but also which syllable is stressed. Ask the student to draw lines between the syllables and then to draw a line under the stressed syllable e.g. *opening:* \o\pen\ing\.

2 Adding 'ed' and 'ing'

When the students are ready ask them to complete the second activity on the worksheet, which requires them to consider very carefully the rules for adding endings.

admitting	happening	opening	visiting
offering	forgetting	transmitting	benefiting
permitting	regretting	permitted	regretted
opened	transmitted	happened	visited
admitted	offered	benefited	occurring

Adding endings to two-syllable words

Name _____

1 Write the focus words in the spaces on this grid.

Look at this word: **open**

It has two syllables. When we say the word we stress the first syllable.

Look at this word: **begin**

It has two syllables. When we say this word we stress the second syllable.

When adding an ending such as **ing** or **ed** to two-syllable words try to remember the following rules:

- if the first syllable is stressed, just add the ending
  (e.g. open → opening)
- if the second syllable is stressed, double the consonant then add the ending
  (e.g. begin → beginning)

2 Without looking at the words on the grid try to use the rules to add the appropriate endings to these words:

root word	ed ending	ing ending
admit	_____	_____
permit	_____	_____
murmur	_____	_____
regret	_____	_____
happen	_____	_____
transmit	_____	_____
offer	_____	_____
benefit	_____	_____

What about the word *forget*? You can add the **ing** ending but you cannot add the **ed** ending. What should you write instead? _____

Recognizing word families

1 Focus on words

● Photocopy this page and the accompanying student worksheet. Discuss the focus words at the bottom of this page with the students. Ask them to write the words in the blank grid on their worksheet. You could dictate the words or, if appropriate, students could copy them from the set below.

● The completed grid on the worksheet, or the one below, could be laminated as a pocket reference card that students could refer to later.

● To analyse the words further, and if appropriate for your students, you could complete the following activities.

Segmenting the words into their phonemes

Explain to the students that they are going to segment some of the words into their separate sounds. Demonstrate with the word *possibly* by drawing lines between the graphemes that represent the separate phonemes: */p/o/ss/i/b/l/y/*. In completing the activity students may come up with different answers from each other but the important part of the activity is in the process of listening to the sounds and observing how they are represented by graphemes.

Splitting the words into their syllables (syllabification)

For most students syllabification is much easier than segmenting. Explain that they are now going to split the words into 'chunks' of sound and give the example of *imagination: \i\mag\in\a\tion*. Can the students hear that the word can be split into five syllables?

2 Sort the words

● When the students are ready ask them to complete the second activity on the worksheet. Help the students to sort the words into three sets and to identify the root word in each set i.e. *image, finite* and *possible*. Discuss how some of the words are created by adding prefixes or suffixes to other words. Specifically look at the word *definitely* which provides a good example of adding the suffix **ly** – many students are tempted to add **ley** instead.

image	indefinite	impossible	define
imaginary	possibly	finite	imaginable
definitely	imaginative	indefinitely	infinity
imagination	possible	definite	imagine
possibility	definition	imagery	impossibility

Recognizing word families

1 Write the focus words in the spaces on this grid.

2 Sort the words from the grid into three sets. All the words in each set should be related to each other. Draw a ring around the word in each set that you think is the 'root' word.

Try to write a sentence using a word from each set.

_____

_____

_____

Adding the prefix ir

1 Focus on words

- Photocopy this page and the accompanying student worksheet. Discuss the focus words at the bottom of this page with the students. Ask them to write the words in the blank grid on their worksheet. You could dictate the words or, if appropriate, students could copy them from the set below.

- The completed grid on the worksheet, or the one below, could be laminated as a pocket reference card that students could refer to later.

- Remind the students that a letter string placed at the front of an existing word to create a new word is called a prefix. Ask them to identify the role of the prefix **ir**. Can they see that adding this prefix creates a word of opposite meaning, i.e. an antonym. Noticing that the prefix is added to the complete word helps with spelling the new word – adding **ir** to the front of *regular*, for example, creates the word *irregular* and it can be seen that the new word has a double letter **r** because the **r** from each part is kept.

- To analyse the words further, and if appropriate for your students, you could complete the following activities.

  Segmenting the words into their phonemes
  Explain to the students that they are going to segment some of the words into their separate sounds. Demonstrate with the word *religious* by drawing lines between the graphemes that represent the separate phonemes: /r/e/l/i/g/iou/s/. Is the grapheme **iou** just one phoneme or is it two? Questions such as this help the students to focus on the structure of the words.

  Splitting the words into their syllables (syllabification)
  For most students syllabification is much easier than segmenting. Explain that they are now going to split the words into 'chunks' of sound and give the example of *irrelevant: \ir\rel\e\vant*. Can the students hear that the word can be split into four syllables?

2 Writing opposites

- When the students are ready ask them to complete the second activity on the worksheet, which asks them to look closely at the words again by considering pairs of antonyms. The students are encouraged to think about other words that can be made into antonyms and how different prefixes are added to different words to achieve this.

rational	irrational	regular	irregular
relevant	irrelevant	religious	irreligious
removable	irremovable	replaceable	irreplaceable
responsible	irresponsible	reversible	irreversible
redeemable	irredeemable	resistible	irresistible

Adding the prefix ir

Name _____

1 Write the focus words in the spaces on this grid.

2 Cover the grid so that you are not tempted to look at the words then write the opposite of each word shown below by adding or removing the prefix **ir**.

irrational _____ replaceable _____

regular _____ irresponsible _____

relevant _____ reversible _____

irreligious _____ irredeemable _____

irremovable _____ resistible _____

Now write the opposites of the words below by adding a prefix to the front of each one. You won't be able to use the same prefix for each word!

possible _____ necessary _____

direct _____ approve _____

modest _____ understand _____

List seven prefixes that can be used to create opposites.

_____ _____ _____ _____ _____ _____

Try to write a sentence containing as many words as possible that start with these prefixes.

_____

_____

_____

Alphabet speed sheet

Name _____

Sometimes you will need to use a dictionary to look up the spellings of words. You need to know your alphabet really well. Here is a fun activity for practising alphabet speed.

Join the letters in alphabetical order as fast as you can. Time yourself.

D E A R S L U K V C F O B Q N Z M J I T Y P W H G X

Teacher's Notes

This activity can be great fun when used in the form of a friendly competition. Students can all start at the same time and try to be first to finish. Alternatively, a student could complete the task on two or three occasions trying to beat her/his personal time.